CANARIES

Hamlyn
PET CARE
Handbooks

CANARIES

J. G. Scott

HAMLYN

Published by
The Hamlyn Publishing Group Limited
Bridge House, 69 London Road
Twickenham, Middlesex TW1 3SB, England
and distributed for them by
Octopus Distribution Services Limited
Rushden, Northamptonshire NN10 9RZ, England

First published 1987

ISBN 0 600 55135 0

Some of the material in this book
is reproduced from other books published
by The Hamlyn Publishing Group Ltd.

Printed in Hong Kong by Mandarin Offset

Contents

Introduction

Canaries were introduced by Spanish explorers into Europe towards the end of the 15th century from the Azores, Madeira and, as the name implies, the Canary Islands. The wild canary is a small yellowish-green serin, and as it lacks the bright colours of many native European finches, its initial popularity was probably due more to its ability to thrive in captivity, than to its appearance.

The Germans, however, were quick to appreciate that the canary's song could be developed and improved and as variations in colour appeared in domesticated stocks, giving rise to clear yellow and yellow-and-green marked birds, so the trade in pet canaries from the Continent into England increased.

In 1709 Hervieux, the superintendent of the aviaries of the Duchesse de Berry in France, named 29 different types of canary in the *Traité des serins de Canarie*. It is apparent however that Hervieux was describing variations in plumage, rather than true breeding varieties, and although mutations had already occurred in the original green stock (cinnamon and crested birds are mentioned) it is not until 1762 that there are clear indications that breeders were favouring one type or colour of canary in preference to all others, with the aim of fixing these different characteristics by selective breeding.

In that year Thomas Hope of London published the *Bird Fancier's Necessary Companion and Sure Guide*, in which he wrote of certain types of canary being 'the most esteemed according to the reigning fancy amongst breeders' and that these birds were 'from a breed which a few years ago was brought hither from France, but since much improved in colour and beauty by English breeders'. This improvement, Hope claims, was done by 'pairing proper coloured cocks with hens in breeding'.

Although nearly a century would elapse before Darwin published his theory of evolution and even longer before Mendel's findings on genetics became known, it seems that groups of working men in England were already aware that distinct breeds of canaries could be established by selective matings carried out under controlled conditions. No records exist of these early fanciers. They are likely to have been people who had little contact with other breeders beyond their own immediate circle, for travel in the 18th and early 19th centuries was a rare luxury. Their activities were probably limited to meetings held in a local hostelry, climaxed annually by a show at the same venue, at which the merits of their birds would be assessed.

They were nevertheless true pioneers in the breeding of pedigree stock, and there are clear indications that separate varieties of canary had evolved by the early years of the 19th century. By then the hobby of keeping canaries was no doubt given impetus by the growth of industrialization and the drift of farm workers, accustomed to handling livestock, from the comparative isolation of the countryside, into towns. Confirmation of

Canaries were very popular pets in Victorian households where they were kept in wooden and wire cages

such progress is contained in an article published in the *Illustrated London News* of 12 December 1846, which described and portrayed in detail the London Fancy canary and the four societies in the metropolis that catered for the breed's interests.

Thereafter, with the startling improvement in communications following the growth of the railway network, progress was rapid and in 1859 a bird show was held at the Crystal Palace in London at which 14 classes were provided for entries from five distinct varieties. By now cage bird societies were springing up in all the main towns in Britain and in response to a demand for information, books on the breeding and exhibition of canaries, including some of the most lavish ever published, were appearing.

At the same time, breeding canaries for sale as pets had become a cottage industry. By the early part of the Victorian era, therefore, separate breeds of canary had been established by fanciers, who had formed societies through which they competed against one another as exhibitors, while the pet singing canary (bred purely for its singing ability) in its wire cage had become an integral part of Victorian households.

The rise in popularity of the canary continued unabated throughout the 19th century and remained unchallenged until the 1920s, when the budgerigar began to attract attention as an exhibition bird. This newcomer from Australia added a new dimension to the cage bird fancy and its ability to learn to repeat simple phrases, together with its playful behaviour, made it a serious rival to the singing canary as a pet, thereby reducing the market that canary fanciers had previously enjoyed for their surplus stock.

The features that gave rise to the popularity of the canary have not, however, changed; indeed the introduction of new colours, and the development of fresh breeds, have provided a diversity of types that the earliest fanciers could not have envisaged. Despite the enormous increase in the range of leisure activities and entertainments in recent years, few towns of any size are without a cage bird society, whose membership invariably includes many canary fanciers, and the pet canary remains a firm favourite.

Choosing and buying

When choosing a canary as a pet, it must be remembered that a hen canary, though indistinguishable in appearance from its mate, cannot sing and is therefore less desirable and should cost much less than a cock bird. Some hens may warble softly, but there is no mistaking the vigorous song of a cock with its head held high and throat throbbing. A newly acquired bird may take two or three days to settle down; any healthy canary sold as a cock which has failed to sing within this period must give rise to doubts as to its sex.

Suitable breeds The breed and colour of canary you choose is a matter of personal preference. All canaries have the same basic characteristics and apart from the Roller, which has been developed for the quality of its

Young pet Border canary being held by its owner

CANARIES

Canaries are quite happy if kept singly; to keep groups of them you need a sizable aviary

song rather than its appearance and is therefore very superior in this respect to its counterparts, they will repay their owners with their bright plumage and active movements and in the case of cock birds, cheerful trills.

The smaller breeds such as the Border Fancy, Fife Fancy, Gloster, Red Factor or Roller, or crosses between them, are most suitable as pets and are best purchased from breeders who have birds which fall below exhibition standard for disposal.

Nowadays very few canaries are bred exclusively for the pet trade and those offered in pet shops are almost invariably the surplus stocks of canary fanciers. Canaries breed in the spring and summer months and moult in late summer and early autumn. The best time to buy a bird is therefore in the period after the moult is complete and when stocks are at their highest.

At this time a current year's bird will be between three and five months old and will have successfully got through the trying stage of adolescence when losses are most likely to occur. It will, however, be young enough to adapt easily to life as a family pet.

Healthy birds If possible, a young bird should always be selected. Canaries have a life expectancy of from seven to nine years. There is no certain guide to age, but the condition of the legs and feet, which are smooth in a juvenile and grow progressively rougher and scalier with the years, gives some indication. A fit bird will be tight and clean in feather, with bright eyes and active movements. You should avoid any in poor feather, which are soiled near the vent, wheeze, or sit puffed up on the perch.

Cages for pet canaries

The choice of cage is important, as it will become the canary's permanent home; preference should therefore be

An alert bright-eyed young canary is the best choice as a pet

given to those of simple design which are spacious and easy to keep clean. A wide selection is available and one made of wire and rectangular in shape is preferable to the tall round type that are more suitable for budgerigars and similar species which have a tendency to climb up and down the bars.

Cage fittings The minimum requirements are a door which opens outwards and allows the owner's hand to reach all parts of the interior, a perch at each end (midway up the sides) with two more near the floor to enable the bird to perch near the seed and water containers and a tray covering the cage bottom which can be easily removed to facilitate cleaning. To prevent seed husks and grit from being scattered, modern cages often have a wire top fitted on to a moulded plastic base extending 8–10 cm (3–4 in) upwards; older types overcome this problem with glass or clear plastic panels at floor level.

A pet canary does not need toys or mirrors to keep it

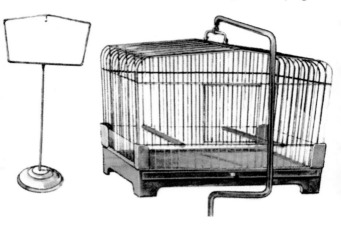

Rectangular cages are more suitable for keeping canaries than tall round ones

amused. The only additional cage fitments required are a bath to be clipped on to the outside of the open cage door; one or two finger feeders to push between the cage wires when providing titbits; clips to hold a piece of cuttlefish and greenstuffs; a small bowl for grit; and a supply of paper sheets, sanded or otherwise, to use as floor covering. If the perches provided are round and made of hard wood or plastic, they can with advantage to the bird's comfort be replaced with lengths of oval shaped softwood.

Location Canaries are very adaptable creatures but they should not be subjected to widely fluctuating temperatures or draughts. These considerations must be taken into account when deciding where the cage will stand or hang.

A corner of a room away from the door and where some, but not too much, direct sunlight can be expected, is perhaps best. It is also sensible to provide a cloth cover to darken the cage in winter evenings, before the artificial lighting is switched on. Greater flexibility in positioning the cage can be gained by the use of a free standing support with a weighted base.

General care

Feeding

Few pets are so easy and inexpensive to cater for as canaries. Their principal food is seed and it is possible, though not desirable, to keep a canary in good health on nothing more than hard seed and water.

Seed mixes Not all seeds are suitable of course, and experience has shown that a mixture of four parts 'white Spanish' to one part 'rubsen rape' forms an excellent staple diet. White Spanish (sometimes called canary seed) is white and oval-shaped and rich in carbohydrates but deficient in fats, whereas rubsen rape, a small round reddish-coloured seed, is very oily. This staple seed mixture should be provided at all times and may be thought of as a canary's bread and butter.

However, birds, like human beings, welcome variety and canaries being no exception will take, with varying degrees of readiness, many other seeds. These include niger, hemp, teazle, linseed and maw and for the small quantities needed for a single pet bird, they can best be provided by purchasing a packet of a proprietary condition seed mixture, and given to the canary in a small finger feeder two or three times a week. Seed should always be plump, clean to the touch and free from dust or a musty smell.

Fresh foods In addition, canaries are very fond of greenstuffs, such as watercress and lettuce, as well as seeding grasses and many common weeds, from which they extract seeds in a ripe or unripened state. Favourite weeds are dandelion (young leaves, roots and seeding heads), chickweed (the whole plant), 'rats-tails' (the seeding heads of the greater plantain) and sowthistle (seeding heads). Greenstuffs of all types can be offered in moderation as they come into season, but they must be fresh and any pieces left uneaten should be removed from the cage. Care must also be taken to see that the source of supply is not contaminated. In winter a piece of raw

Shepherd's purse (1), marram grass (2), sow thistle (3), plantain (4), fescue grass (5) and young dandelion (6) are all suitable food for canaries

carrot, sweet apple or half a Brussels sprout, make excellent substitutes.

Other foods Canaries also relish a small amount of 'soft food' occasionally. Proprietary brands of soft food consist of biscuit meal enriched with vitamins and other additives such as dried egg yolk or powdered milk. Some brands are dry and require the addition of water; others have been blended with honey or a similar ingredient and can be fed direct from the packet.

A source of calcium, important for bone structure, can be provided by a piece of cuttlefish bone clipped to the cage wires for the bird to peck. For drinking, cold water straight from the tap is perfectly suitable and must always be available.

Grits Although canaries husk the seeds they eat before swallowing them, some kernels are hard and need to be broken down in their gizzards, prior to digestion. To

17

facilitate this process, canaries, in common with other seed-eating birds, pick up tiny pieces of grit from the ground when feeding. Packets of suitable mineralized grits can be purchased, but clean sea or river sand is just as good and a small pot full of whatever type is obtained should be provided.

Day-to-day care

Pet canaries appreciate and will become accustomed to a regular routine. Every day therefore the seed pot should be removed at a set time, preferably in the early morning, and the husks blown off before the pot is refilled with the staple seed mixture; the water container must also be emptied daily, thoroughly cleaned and replenished with fresh water. Every second or third day a little of the mixed condition seed can be given in the finger feeder, and once a week a similar amount of soft food.

The bird will quickly learn to anticipate these offerings, especially the mixed seed and soft food and will become tame to the extent of coming to the end of the perch as the finger feeder is inserted. Its confidence in its owner will be further strengthened if greenstuffs such as a sprig of chickweed or a seeding dandelion head are proffered by hand; few canaries can resist such delicacies.

Bathing Twice a week, the bath, half filled with cold water, can be hung on the open door of the cage; the enclosed clear plastic type of bath is best as it prevents water from being splashed about – a necessary precaution for canaries are enthusiastic bathers. After the bird has had an opportunity to preen and dry itself, the floor covering should be changed and the sand pot refilled. Perches also become soiled and every two or three weeks they can be removed and washed; a replacement set being kept in reserve for this purpose. At the same time the glass or plastic side panels can be wiped clean.

Territory The temptation to obtain a companion for a pet canary should always be resisted. Canaries have strong territorial instincts and in the confines of a single cage will demonstrate their dislike of intruders by squabbling or fighting vigorously.

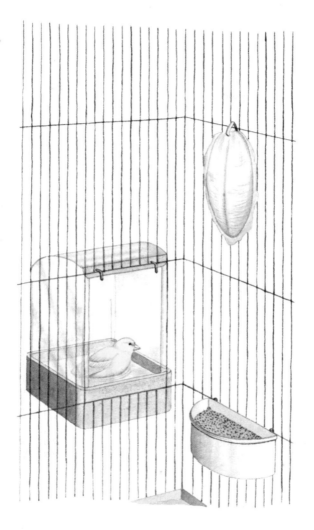

Canaries thoroughly enjoy splashing about in water; a cuttlefish bone hung in the cage provides essential calcium for caged birds

Ailments and moult

A fit young canary, acquired in the autumn after it has completed its juvenile moult, should enjoy several years of active life free from disease; it is also extremely unlikely to suffer injury. This presupposes careful attention on the part of the owner, especially during the annual moult.

Moulting This is a perfectly natural occurrence which takes place in the late summer months, when canaries gradually shed their old feathers and grow new ones. It is, however, a taxing experience and the bird should be kept as quiet and undisturbed as possible, until it has acquired its new plumage. Slightly more generous helpings of mixed seed and soft food will be welcome and a regular supply of seeding grasses and other greenstuffs will intensify the depth of colour in the new feathers. While the bird will look a little ragged and be subdued during this period – cock birds will stop singing – there is no need to worry about its general health and the twice weekly bath should not be withheld.

Soft moult A moult or partial moult out of season is *not* natural and indicates that the bird affected is in poor condition. The usual causes for what is termed a 'soft moult' are incorrect feeding, violent fluctuations in temperature or too much exposure to artificial light, but if the patient is placed in more stable surroundings and given a properly balanced diet, it should soon recover.

Fractures Broken wings and legs require veterinary attention. In the case of a leg the broken bone end needs to be re-aligned and splinted into position. Leg fractures are splinted using an inelastic adhesive plaster, with the leg being sandwiched between two pieces which are then trimmed to size. Quiet and strict isolation are again essential during the four to six weeks' convalescence.

A canary looking less sleek than usual in late summer is undergoing its annual moult

Occasionally a bird may trap its foot and sprain or break a toe and will suffer discomfort and spend a day or two hopping about on one leg before recovering.

A wing is difficult to splint and it may be best to let nature take its course and hope that the wing will knit of its own accord.

Toenail growth As a canary gets older, its toenails will grow longer and may need to be trimmed. The bird should be held firmly in one hand and the tips of the nails cut with a sharp pair of scissors, care being taken to cut below the vein which can be clearly seen as a thin red line in each nail, when the bird's foot is held up to the light.

Parasites For all practical purposes internal parasites are not encountered in Britain among canaries kept in cages;

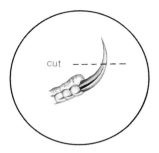

When trimming canaries' claws it is vital to avoid the blood vessel, which can be made out on close inspection

external parasites in the form of lice or mites are relatively common, however, and if left unchecked will weaken infected birds. They comprise two types: those that live on the bird and eat feather and skin; and those that hide in crevices in the cage and at the ends of the perches during the day, crawling out at night from their hiding places to suck the bird's blood. A single bird in isolation in a clean wire cage should not be troubled; if pests are found, however, there are many safe modern insecticides in aerosol or powder form which will quickly eradicate them if the birds and cages are thoroughly treated according to the manufacturer's instructions.

Illnesses A number of diseases can affect pet canaries, of which some of the general signs in birds are listed below:

1 Singing reduced or stopped other than during moulting

2 Voracious appetite

3 Faeces change in character. They may become watery or change colour

4 The bird's attitude changes. It becomes listless, sleepy, less active and may stop flying

5 The bird's appearance changes. It will sit with ruffled feathers and discharges may be evident around the beak and eyes, or feathers around the vent may be soiled

6 If the bird has a respiratory disease its breathing will become noisy with rattles and wheezes.

If any of these symptoms persists you should take your canary to the vet and when doing so it will help if you follow these guidelines:–

1 Take the bird in its own cage

2 Do not clean out the cage, but take it as it is to the vet so that he can see the droppings etc

3 Before leaving home empty the water dish or drinker and replace, to prevent spillage during transit.

4 Cover the cage and especially in colder weather wrap it in a blanket, to keep the bird warm, free of draughts and calm.

5 If the canary is weak, injured or showing nervous signs, remove the swings and perches.

6 Take any medicine or vitamin supplement you have been giving the bird.

Breeding

Keeping a pet canary often arouses interest in the pastime of breeding for exhibition. If you decide on this, fine: but first it is important to consider what is involved, for keeping any form of livestock imposes responsibilities upon the owner, and canaries require daily attention. To attend to one bird takes only a few minutes, but a number can make considerable demands on your spare time, especially during the breeding season, and this should not be forgotten in your initial enthusiasm to obtain stock.

Canaries require the correct accommodation for breeding. A pet bird is best kept on its own and will thrive in an all-wire cage in the living room, but if you are to take up breeding you will have to make totally different arrangements. These will depend to a great extent on the number of birds you keep.

Newly hatched baby birds are noisy, demanding and somewhat unattractive

Acquiring your first stock

Sound advice to a newcomer is to start with not more than four or five pairs of one variety. The choice of variety is a personal matter and once a decision has been taken, it is sensible to approach an experienced breeder in the autumn, when stock will be available, and seek his advice.

The great majority of established fanciers have a reputation to maintain and will not take advantage of inexperience; on the contrary, they will select properly matched pairs that should be capable of producing typical specimens of the chosen breed and start the newcomer in the right direction.

Novices cannot be expected to appreciate the finer show points, for this can only come with experience, but you should remember that sick birds are never a good investment, whatever their pedigree. Secondly, canaries have a comparatively short breeding span, so young stock is much to be preferred, even if it may cost more.

When you are starting up, you have no use for expensive prize birds. There is a recognized acceptable price for a 'stock pair' of each breed, and as a newcomer you should not pay above that until you have gained more experience.

Fitting up a bird room

The location of your bird room is the all-important factor. If space outdoors is not available, a spare bedroom or attic with a southerly aspect will be satisfactory, providing it can be shut off from the rest of the house; but a separate outdoor building is always much better. This can be of brick or wooden construction, and as it will involve the largest single financial outlay, it is essential that you make a choice that you will be happy with.

It is also important to ensure that the structure complies with local planning and building by-law regulations and that you have obtained all the necessary clearances or consents from the local council, before you begin construction. At this stage no harm is done, and future misunderstandings may be avoided, by letting your neighbours know what is proposed.

A brick structure has the advantage of strength and permanence, though in a mobile society this latter consideration could prove to be a drawback. The choice of timber is, therefore, usually the wiser investment, especially if the building is constructed in sections, which will allow it to be extended, or dismantled and re-constructed later.

Specifications There are firms that specialize in making bird rooms for sale, or you can hire a local builder to carry out your own specifications. A bird room can be expensive, but do not be tempted to purchase a flimsy garden hut on the grounds of economy. This will not stand up to the daily use you will need to make of it.

The basic requirement to house a stud of up to ten breeding pair of canaries is a plain shed, 3.5 m long and 2 m wide (12 ft × 6 ft 6 in). In height it should slope from 2.5 m at the front to 2.15 m at the rear (8–7 ft). Constructed of 2.5 cm (1 in) tongued and grooved planking, on a 10 × 7.5 cm (4 × 3 in) main frame, such a structure will give a lifetime of service and, if lined with hardboard, will provide protection from the extremes of summer heat and winter cold.

Adequate natural light is important and if possible the windows, which should be on the front of the building, should face south or south-east, to take advantage of the early morning sun. Windows that can be opened in fine weather are preferable and should be fitted with fine-mesh wire grilles, to restrain possible escapes and exclude intruders.

Air and access Provide ventilation at both floor and ceiling level: the whole structure should stand some 30 cm (1 ft) above the ground on concrete or brick pillars. This will allow air to circulate freely around the building, permit cats to pass by underneath without undue difficulty and prevent rodents from taking up residence.

The door is best placed centrally at the front, to allow you to use the whole of the back and sides for cages. Canaries themselves do not need artificial lighting or heating, and if you decide to install these for your own convenience, enabling you to attend to your birds in winter during the hours of darkness, use them sparingly.

For electric lights, fit a dimmer switch to provide a period of twilight during which the birds can become

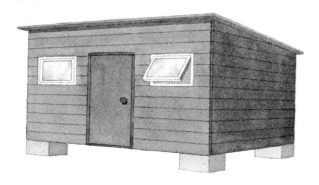

Above: *a bird room should stand well clear of the ground;*
below: *cages can be stacked along three walls of a bird room*

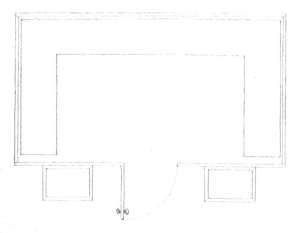

accustomed to the change when the lights go on or off.
Electricity is the best source of power; gas is most
unsuitable and if an oil heater is used, follow the
manufacturer's instructions to the letter and always
maintain the apparatus in perfect condition.

The roof of the hut must of course be made waterproof,
with a good quality roofing felt.

Cages for canary breeding

A canary cage need be no more than an oblong wooden box, with a wire front. Although you can buy these from specialist firms, making one presents few problems even to the average handyman, especially as standard-size wire fronts are readily available and you can buy the wood already cut to size.

Multiple breeding cages

Simplicity and uniformity are the key to cage design: leave out embellishments. A row of single cages is of limited use, because each one can house only one or two birds, and cannot be extended. Breeders therefore

A breeding canary should be provided with soft material which she can use to build a nest

normally use double or treble cages. These are open-fronted boxes, fitted with two or three cage-fronts and one or two movable slides which you insert to form two or three separate compartments. These cages should be constructed to take a standard cage-front of 40 × 30 cm (16 × 12 in) and be 35 cm deep and 40 cm high (14 × 15 in).

Double breeding cages are used when a pair of canaries is kept together during the breeding season; treble breeders when one cock bird is run alternatively with two hens, each of which will occupy one of the outer compartments. After the breeding season, with the slides removed, these cages are useful for weaning young stock, or providing roomy flights for hens.

Fittings and perches

Cage fitments should be simple, and here again uniformity is desirable. The cross rail that supports the cage front is fixed some 2 cm ($\frac{3}{4}$ in) above the floor and the space beneath allows the cage to be cleaned out. Some owners provide a tray to cover the cage floor that can be slid in and out, but it is just as effective, and simpler, to insert a strip of wood which fits the opening and can be removed to allow the soiled floor covering to be taken out.

Two perches of oval softwood are sufficient for each cage, placed from front to back on either side of the cage door. The wire front will be provided with a sliding door, and openings for the seed hopper and drinker. Glass 'top hat' shaped drinkers are best, held to the outside of the front by a wire loop. Use clear plastic seed hoppers.

Built-in cages

If you have the cages built into the bird room, as an integral part of the structure, this has many advantages. These include cheapness, as the inner wall of the room forms the back of each cage. Building them in simply consists of fitting shelves at the appropriate heights, and partitioning the space between them at intervals determined by the length of the cage-fronts chosen. Cages constructed in this fashion allow you even more scope to provide flights of differing lengths, when you take out the partitions.

Pairing and nesting

Having erected and fitted out a bird room and acquired stock, the fancier will look forward to the breeding season with keen anticipation.

Winter feeding and care During the winter, cock birds are best caged separately, while hens enjoy exercise together in flights or stock cages. This is a comparatively quiet period, and the birds should have a plain seed diet of four parts white Spanish to one part rubsen rape, with a little soft food and mixed seeds offered on alternate days twice a week.

Brussels sprouts and raw carrot will also be appreciated and, as soon as they appear in early spring, collect dandelion leaves together with the roots; these are an excellent conditioner for your canaries.

Early spring As the days lengthen, the cocks will begin to sing lustily and the hens will become more and more active, squabbling among themselves and carrying in their beaks any pieces of material that they find on the cage floor. Their excitement and impatience are contagious, but you should be cautious and, tempering enthusiasm with good sense, delay breeding operations until there are reasonable prospects of settled weather.

When this occurs each hen should be placed in the breeding cage reserved for her, with her intended mate in the adjoining compartment, separated by the dividing slide. Canaries display strong territorial instincts at this period of the year, and hens require privacy for their nests, while the cock birds will defend their territory and their mate against all intruders.

The start of breeding

If a pair are ready to breed, they will quickly try to make each other's acquaintance. At this stage leave the slide slightly withdrawn, so that the birds can see their partners, and you can observe their reactions.

Some canaries are slower than others in coming into breeding condition; they should never, however, be 'stoked up' with a sudden rush of delicacies; providing they have been looked after properly throughout the winter, all that is now required is spring itself, with its longer hours of daylight and warmer temperatures.

Courtship feeding Although the cock and hen in their adjoining cages are separated, you will start noticing after a day or two that the cock begins to feed his mate through the slight gap left at the back of the slide. This means that a 'pair bond' has been established, and you can remove the slide altogether. Mating may not take place immediately and there may even be a little bickering, but usually the pair will quickly settle down.

Nest pans These are purchased ready-made from your specialist supplier. Hang a nest pan between the perches at the back of one cage. It is usual to stick a piece of felt, cut to shape, inside the pan to provide a 'key' on which the hen will build the nest. Canary hens build a finch-type nest – a framework of grasses lined with soft material – so you need to supply a handful of hay and some soft stuff, such as cotton wool or cow hair.

Many hens play about with the material at first, or start nest-building only to pull the results of their labour to pieces when nearing completion. This may continue for a few days, but normally within a fortnight the nest should be built and the hen ready to lay. Four or five eggs comprise a normal clutch.

Dummy eggs To try and ensure that all these eggs hatch out within a few hours of one another, it is customary to remove the first three as they are laid each morning and replace them with dummies. Store the real eggs in a box lined with cotton wool.

On the evening of the third day remove the dummies and dust the inside of the nest with a safe insect powder, then replace the real eggs. The hen will then start to incubate.

Hatching

If the cock proves too lively and harasses his mate – a common occurrence – he should be shut off in the adjoining cage. Meanwhile the hen will sit tightly on her

Above: *commercially available nest pans provide a base in which the breeding canary builds her nest;* **below:** *the hen sits on the eggs almost constantly after she has laid them until they hatch twelve to fifteen days later*

nest, leaving only briefly to feed and drink. Her diet need be no more than the staple seed mixture of canary and rape plus cold water, but on the evening of the twelfth day of incubation a small amount of soft food can be offered in a feeding drawer, in anticipation of the chicks hatching out on the following day.

If the weather has been cold or the hen has not sat tightly, hatching can be delayed two or three days. Any eggs that have not hatched out after this time are either infertile (clear eggs) or the embryo has died (dead in the shell).

Check the eggs for fertility, on the sixth or seventh day of incubation, by holding each one between thumb and forefinger in front of a strong light. The infertile ones will appear translucent; fertile eggs will be dark in appearance.

Infertile eggs indicate that successful mating has not taken place, or that one or both of the breeding pair have not been fully fit. A dead embryo may be due to a natural weakness in the chick, or because the inner membrane of the egg shell may have developed a puncture, preventing development by dehydration.

The most usual cause, however, is the hen leaving the nest and allowing the eggs to chill. This can occur at night if a hen is disturbed and cannot find her way back on to the nest, until first light the next morning. If you have installed artificial lights, therefore, you should never turn these on and off in the bird room at night, once breeding has begun.

You have to expect a certain percentage of 'clear eggs' and 'dead in the shell', and providing they are the exception rather than the rule, there is no need to worry unduly. Hens with clear clutches should be allowed to sit for the full 13 days of incubation before their nests are removed. Such hens and any others that have failed to hatch chicks, for whatever reason, should be given a few days' rest, before being re-mated.

The young birds

Foods for chicks

You can buy a proprietary brand of soft food for your chicks, or if you wish you can make your own. To do so, take a handful of dry biscuit meal, the yolk of one hard boiled egg, a teaspoonful of a high-protein invalid food, a few drops of cod liver oil and a sprinkling of maw seed. Moisten with cold water and mix to a crumbly consistency. If you have only three or four pairs of canaries, this will initially be one day's supply. Make it up in time for the morning feed and store the unused portion in an airtight container for the midday and evening feeds.

Additional food For the first two or three days of their lives, canary chicks require very little soft food and it is wasteful to provide too much. By the fifth day, however, the nestlings will be clamouring for food and their mother will be spending more and more time away from them looking for extra food with which to satisfy their hunger. Greenstuffs – seeding chickweed and partially ripened dandelion heads – are invaluable at this time and will be eagerly taken.

In addition offer the hen a feeder full of soaked seed – teazle and rubsen rape – once a day. The mixture should be covered with cold water for at least 24 hours and then well rinsed in a sieve under a tap before being offered.

Keeping clean Up to the eighth or ninth day, the hen and the cock, if he is present, will keep the nest clean by removing or swallowing the chicks' droppings, which to facilitate the process are contained in a gelatinous sac. Afterwards the youngsters will be large enough to defecate over the edge of the nest pan.

If the cock bird has been kept separate, this is a good time to reunite him with his mate, so that he can help her in feeding their offspring.

A nestful of youngsters and their parents within a comparatively confined space pose hygiene problems; droppings are copious, while soft food and soaked seed as well as greenstuffs tend to be scattered and, if left on the cage floor, will become sour, especially in warm weather. It is impracticable to remove every trace of spilt food, but the cage must be kept sweet, and this can best be done by providing a really thick floor covering of dry sawdust.

Fledging

By the time the nestlings are 19 days old they will be smaller editions of their parents. The youngsters will spend a good deal of time testing their wings before actually leaving the nest, but once out some will be reluctant to return. A good cock bird is a great asset at this time and will largely take over the role of feeding the chicks, allowing the hen to get on with the job of building a second nest.

A Border canary feeding its voracious newly hatched young

A new nest pan should be provided and as the hen's building urge will be as great as ever, a plentiful supply of nesting material must be available, or she may obtain it by plucking her first brood.

The chicks will soon learn to fend for themselves and at about the age of 21 days they can be shut off in one compartment of the cage away from the new nest, with a small space left at the back of the slide through which the

Young canaries are still fed by their parents when they are comparatively large

parent birds will continue feeding. As soon as one member of the brood starts to feed itself however, the others will quickly follow suit and the youngsters can be considered to be self-supporting.

Segregation At this stage they should be placed in groups of five or six, in a roomy cage of the double breeder type, with the perches placed low down and the floor well covered with dry sawdust. The foods on which they have been reared should continue to be offered but after two or three more weeks they will commence to crack and eat hard seed. Soft food should still be given, but less and less will be eaten as the young birds spend more time at the seed hopper.

The weaning period, allied to the first juvenile moult, is the most critical period of a canary's life and the age when most losses occur. The fancier should remember, therefore, that young canaries, like all young creatures, have yet to gain their full strength and vigour and are more susceptible to disease, disturbance and unsuitable foods, than adult stock.

Exhibiting

Like the owners of any other form of livestock, canary fanciers have developed, by selection, breeds which differ widely from each other in size and form. To canary fanciers breeds such as the Yorkshire, Lizard, Norwich and Border Fancy represent a great advance on the original stock. Maintaining a recognized breed of canary to an agreed standard of excellence provides an opportunity for many people to practise the art of 'stockmanship' and test the merits of the progeny produced in competition.

Clubs and organizations

In many countries, organizations for showing canaries have been in existence for a long time. They usually comprise a network of specialist societies whose main function is to lay down the recognized standard for each breed and to appoint judges to maintain that standard.

Alongside these there are numerous regional and local associations which cater either for all breeds or for one specific breed. By holding regular meetings and staging shows, these local clubs provide the main points of contact for fanciers. Shows can vary from small club events held in a village or church hall, with an entry of 200 to 300 exhibits, to exhibitions in national stadiums where you may see 6,000 canaries or more.

Whatever the show and wherever it is held, exactly the same standards will apply, both for presentation and assessment.

Breed standards

The criteria laid down for a particular breed are of course merely a reflection of personal preferences or fancies (hence the word 'fancier') of the breeders concerned and a newcomer to the 'fancy' is similarly influenced by his likes and dislikes, in the choice of a breed to keep. There is no rationale other than personal choice. In making this choice, as a newcomer you should realize that to be successful, you must stage birds displaying the qualities that your fellow exhibitors consider desirable, and that have been incorporated in the standard for the breed.

This is an important consideration. In some kinds of competitive livestock breeding you are at liberty to follow your personal preferences and your animal or bird may still win if it can achieve a certain standard of performance. The colour or configuration of a racing pigeon, for example, are unimportant if the bird can beat its rivals in a race. But with canaries, success (except for the Roller or singing canary), depends entirely upon the judge's opinion of your bird's appearance.

Therefore study the standard laid down for your breed and learn to recognize a good exhibition bird. Drawings and descriptions are helpful, but there is no substitute for visiting shows and seeing, 'in the feather', the best canaries on view.

It is not practicable in this book to include the standards and scales of points for all breeds. You can obtain copies of these from the specialist societies concerned; but to give you an idea of what is involved, we shall give one example of an official scale of points. This shows the order of priority in which a judge assesses the various qualities of an exhibit on the show bench before him. The breed we have chosen is the Lizard Canary:

Scale of points for Lizard Canaries

Spangles	For regularity and distinctness	25
Feather quality	For tightness and silkiness	15
Ground colour	For depth and evenness	10
Breast	For extent and regularity of rowings	10
Wings and tail	For neatness and darkness	10
Cap	For neatness and shape	10
Covert feathers	For lacings	5
Eyelash	For regularity and clarity	5
Beak, legs and feet	For darkness	5
Steadiness and staging		5
		100

From this list you can tell two things immediately: (1) that the most important show characteristic for this breed of canary is called 'Spangles', and (2) that without viewing an exhibition Lizard, or at least reading a fuller description of its show qualities, the bare details provided in the scale of points are of limited value to a novice exhibitor.

Spangles of a Lizard The term 'spangles' (or 'spangling') refers to the series of small black markings on a Lizard's back, formed by overlapping feathers, which because of their supposed resemblance to the scales of the reptile, give the breed its name.

Each spangle should be clear and distinct and as black as possible, extending from the base of the cap, in perfectly straight parallel rows, down the back. In the best specimens, these markings are startlingly clear; few birds, however, attain this high standard and a judge normally has to choose between less than perfect exhibits.

While a Lizard which is seriously deficient in spangling has little chance of success, no matter how good its other features, the judge's overall assessment will cover the merits of its other features and so you must be aware of their relative values, and of what to look for in a good exhibition bird. This involves having a clear mental picture of the 'ideal' which we shall now describe. To be specific, we shall quote verbatim from the official standard for the Clear Capped Gold variety of the Lizard breed of canary.

Description of ideal Clear Capped Gold Lizard canary

The bird should not exceed 12.5 cm (5 in) in length, neither too stout nor too slim. It stands quietly and confidently on the perch at an angle of 45°. The ground colour is uniform in depth and is a rich golden bronze, entirely free from suggestion of any other shade.

The spangling is clear and distinct, each individual spangle being clear of another. It extends from the edge of the cap in perfectly straight lines to the wing coverts, each succeeding spangle being progressively larger than the one nearer the neck.

The feather quality is of conspicuous silkiness, the feathers being close and tight with no suggestion of coarseness or looseness.

The breast is round and fairly full without giving any appearance of stoutness. The rowings are clear and distinct one from another, and are linable.

The wing feathers are compact and held closely to the body. Their tips meet in a straight line down the centre of the back. They are so dark (except on the extreme edges) as to appear almost black.

The tail is narrow, straight and neat, with feathers of the quality and colour of the wing feathers.

The head is fairly large, round and full on the top.

The cap extends from the base of the upper mandible to the base of the skull and is oval in shape with a clearly defined edge. It is clear of the eye, being separated therefrom by the eyelash, which is a clear and well defined line of dark feathers, extending to the base of the upper mandible.
  There are no dark feathers between the cap and the upper mandible. The cap is of a deep golden orange colour and has no blemish of dark or light feather.

The beak, legs and feet are black.

The bird is in perfect condition, quite steady and staged correctly.

Learn from experience This description of an ideal Lizard inevitably raises questions, the answers to which can only come with experience and from specialist books on the subject. Similar considerations apply to all breeds and varieties; broadly speaking, each has one or two features that exhibitors consider to be of major importance, and unless exhibits excel in these, their chances of success are small.
  As a newcomer to exhibiting, therefore, you have to assimilate a great deal of specialist knowledge before you

A show standard Clear Cap Gold Lizard cock

can be confident that your views are in line with those of your competitors; in the final analysis however, it is only by exhibiting your birds and noting how they fare in competition, that you will find out whether or not you have bred and staged the type of exhibits that judges favour.

Show procedures

Exhibiting any form of livestock is governed by strict rules and these must be followed, otherwise an exhibit, irrespective of its merits, will risk disqualification. Canaries are normally exhibited in the late autumn and early winter months, when they have completed the moult and are in perfect feather. Obtain a schedule from the secretary of the society promoting the show and enter your exhibits in the appropriate classes provided. On the morning of the show, or the previous evening, take your exhibits to the show venue in their show cages.

Show cages

Each variety has its own standard type of cage, designed to allow the exhibit to display itself to its best advantage and to allow the judge to examine it carefully and with as little disturbance as possible. The cages are of two types: all wire apart from a wooden base, or a wooden box cage with a wire front; there are variations of these two basic designs for each variety. Show cages are smaller than the normal stock cage and should be used to confine a bird only for the short duration of the show.

Exhibition classes

For exhibition purposes, newcomers are termed novices and compete against one another; after gaining experience and success at this level, they then proceed to champion status and exhibit their birds against other champion exhibitors.

All canaries, even those with green plumage, are termed either yellow or buff. The difference in shade arises from the structure of the feather, which in buff is somewhat larger and softer in texture and displays a slight frosting on the outer margin; this results in a pale lemon tint, whereas yellow feather is much more the colour of a buttercup. The depth of colour varies, but 'buffs' and 'yellows', are generally easy to tell apart.

Your status as a novice or champion, and the choice between yellow and buff colour groups of the birds, together with their age, sex and colour variety, determine

Lizard and Frill canary show cages

a classification that will allow a large number of canaries of the same breed to be split up into groups, or classes, of reasonable size. This allows the judges first to choose class winners and then to select from these the recipients of prizes for best cock, hen, adult, young canary or whatever else may be chosen as a special award.

Colour fed breeds

A further aspect of exhibiting that can be confusing to newcomers is the term 'colour fed'. Until the 1870s fanciers sought to improve the natural colour of their birds by feeding them a wide range of wild seeds and other substances during the moult. It was then found that when very small quantities of capsicums (red peppers) were added to the diet, these imparted an orange tinge to the new plumage, which many exhibitors found attractive. Feeding colour food, as the peppers were named, came to be permitted for certain breeds, which were termed 'colour fed', but strictly prohibited for others.

Improved colouring agents have since been introduced for the colour fed breeds, and provided they are given as directed, immediately before and throughout the moult, you can obtain a very deep shade of orange in the new feathers. The colour foods are all derived from natural substances and there is nothing harmful in such feeding.

Breeds

All breeds of canary exercise a charm that can be fully appreciated only by seeing them, or hearing their song. The brief descriptions of the various breeds given in the following pages can, therefore, do no more than hint at their special characteristics in the broadest outline.

Type Canaries

The expression 'type canaries' indicates birds which are bred primarily for shape, rather than colour, feather pattern, song or posture. They form the most numerous and popular group and as their names imply, are all British in origin.

Left to right: *Dutch Frill, Green Gloster Corona and Ticked Yellow Border canaries*

Although colour is not the main criterion for judging the exhibits, it provides the main method, together with age and sex, of classifying type canaries for exhibition. Three main colour classifications are known as clears, variegated and selfs.

The original yellow (buff) canary produced mutations (called sports). These included cinnamon-marked birds and white canaries with slaty blue markings. As a result of selective breeding from the sports, the colours available today range from clear yellow (buff) and clear white, through every stage of green, cinnamon and blue markings to completely dark green, cinnamon and blue birds (selfs).

Border Fancy The Border Fancy typifies the general concept of what a canary should look like, being of medium size, jaunty in its action and usually clear or lightly variegated in colour. To the exhibitor, however, the Border presents a great challenge, for not only is it the most popular variety and competition is consequently fierce, but considerable skill is needed to combine the many features that make up a well balanced specimen.

The judge looks for a small, round, neat head, a distinct neck, a nice rise to the back and a well rounded chest. Wings should be held closely to the body and the tail tightly folded. Feather quality and depth of natural colour are also very important; the general impression should be that of a beautifully proportioned and lively bird.

Fife Fancy The newest variety, the Fife was developed in the 1960s by fanciers who felt that the Border Fancy was becoming too big and no longer lived up to its old name of the 'Wee Gem'. The Fife is simply a smaller version of the Border and apart from size should resemble it in every detail. It is an extremely attractive bird and an example with good feathers and deep colour will, by its diminutiveness, display a jewel-like quality.

Norwich Unlike the lively Border and Fife, the Norwich is much more sedate in its movements, as befits a bird of rotund proportions. The required qualities are a broad head with a short neck merging imperceptibly into a stout, nicely rounded body. The tail should be short and

Top: *Red Factor;* **above left:** *variegated Border Fancy;*
above right: *self green Roller;* **below:** *Fife Fancy*

the wings well braced. Although its 'bullfinch shape' gives the impression of size, the bird should not exceed 16.5 cm (6½ in) in length. It is customary to colour feed a Norwich for exhibition; this imparts an orange tint to yellow plumage.

Yorkshire The 'Gentleman of the Fancy' or 'Guardsman' are names given to the Yorkshire and allude to its upright stance and swaggering manner. At one time Yorkshires were tall slim birds, and a good specimen was said to be able to pass through a wedding ring. In recent years, however, birds with broad, round heads and wide shoulders have been favoured, and though the essential qualities of stance, smooth feather and nervous energy have been maintained, a much bolder model has resulted. This can be up to 17.5 cm (7 in) in length. Like the Norwich, the Yorkshire is colour fed.

Blue variegated white Yorkshire canary

Crested Canaries

All crested canaries display the same form of circular crest, which radiates from a distinct centre on the top of the head. Crested canaries cannot be truly bred together; the recognized mating is crest × plainhead (non-crested) which gives a 50/50 expectation of both types.

Crest To the late Victorians, the Crest was the 'King of the Fancy' and at the turn of the century was widely kept. It is not so widespread today, but its chief characteristics – a large, drooping crest and solid Norwich type body – have been retained. The crest feathers cannot be too long for exhibition purposes and should radiate downwards below the eyes and cover the beak. The crest-bred or plainhead canary should be a large bird with long head feathers to give it a sulky or browy appearance. Feather quality and colour are of relatively little importance in this breed.

Gloster Fancy The Gloster has to a large extent taken the place formerly occupied by the Crest and is now bred and exhibited in large numbers. It is, however, a much smaller bird – the smaller the better – and its neat daisy crest must not obscure the eyes. Type is also important, the aim being to breed a dainty, lively small bird, that nevertheless conveys an impression of solidity and cobbiness in form. Crested Glosters are known as 'Coronas' and their plainhead mates as 'Consorts'.

Lancashire The Lancashire was developed in the first half of the 19th century and though never numerous or widely kept outside its native English county, it played an important part in the creation of the Crest and Yorkshire. Lancashires are the giants of the canary family: a good specimen exceeds 20 cm (8 in) in length, with a correspondingly massive body, neck and head and bold upright stance.

The Lancashire with a crest is called a 'Coppy', and for perfection its headpiece should be of a horseshoe shape,

Above right: *three parts dark buff Gloster Corona cock;* **right:** *Buff Gloster Consort hen*

The Lancashire (left), the largest variety of canary with an ordinary recessive fawn for comparison of size

displaying long frontal feathers and a smooth back. Only clear-feathered birds or Coppies with grizzled crests are eligible for exhibition.

The breed died out during the Second World War, but has been revived in recent years by crossing Yorkshires with crested canaries.

Singing Canaries

Roller Only the Roller Canary is bred exclusively for its song and this is so superior in sweetness and tone to that of any other variety, that it must be heard to be appreciated. The song comprises a number of 'passages' or 'tours' – Glucke, Bass, Water Roll, Flutes, Bell Roll, etc – and a trained bird will render these on demand, passing effortlessly and without pause from one tour to another.

Scotch Fancy

Belgian canary

Breeding and colour feeding have produced a wide range of canary colours

Roller breeders tend to keep to themselves, for the good reason that if their birds come within earshot of other varieties they may imitate their harsher notes and so be spoilt for exhibition. Colour and form are of no consequence; the only criteria for a good Roller is quality and range of song.

Posture Canaries

This term is used to describe birds which for exhibition purposes can assume an exaggerated stance or posture that differs from their normal carriage. They are not numerous today, but as their names – the Belgian and the Scotch Fancy – imply, they were once the national canaries of their respective countries. Their special posture is a characteristic of the breed and cannot be induced by training.

Belgian This is an ancient breed, developed by town guilds in its native Belgium towards the end of the 18th century. The Belgian is a tall, upright bird with massive shoulders, and displays by thrusting its narrow head and long neck forward to form a right angle with its body and tail, which are held in a perpendicular position. A good bird will show a great deal of nervous energy, gripping the perch firmly while it maintains its stance.

Scotch Fancy Whilst the Belgian's posture is angular in form, the Scotch Fancy is a bird of curves, once known as 'the bird of circle'; head, neck, body and tail form a continuous sweep or halfmoon, with the head and neck well forward and the tail curving underneath the perch. A snake-like head, slender body and long legs and tail are desirable features. The Scotch Fancy is also a bird of movement and should hop briskly from perch to perch, adopting its stance immediately on alighting.

Coloured Canaries

Red Factors are canaries descended from fertile hybrids, bred from crosses between yellow canaries and a South American finch, the black-hooded red siskin. In the immediate post-Second World War years, the aim was simply to produce a true-breeding red canary, that owed its coloration to its genetic make-up rather than to specialized feeding.

Some progress was made, but it was not until a superior proprietary colouring agent was put on the market in the 1960s that deep red orange and apricot canaries appeared on the show bench in large numbers. Increased interest has given rise to mutations, and there is now a wide field for the fancier wishing to specialize in experimental breeding.

Frilled Canaries

Canaries with long curly feathers are widely kept on the Continent, but have not achieved the same popularity elsewhere. There are three main breeds and all have the same pattern of feathering. This consists of: 'the mantle' – back feathers which fall symmetrically over the whole length of the shoulders and back; 'the fins' – side feathers curling upwards to engulf the body; and 'the craw' – feathers which form an incurving shell over the chest. The Parisian is the largest breed, being some 20 cm (8 in) long with a bold upright stance, heavily feathered head and thighs, and long curly toenails. The North Dutch is a smaller and livelier version of the Parisian and differs in having a smooth head, neck and thighs. The third breed – the South Dutch – resembles its northern counterpart in feathering, but instead of an upright stance, adopts the exaggerated posture of the Belgian canary.

Patterned canaries

At one time, breeders of 'type' canaries tended to favour birds with regular markings even though they could exercise no control through pairings, as variegation is variable. Nowadays, little attention is paid to this feature in general. There is, however, one breed – the Lizard – which is judged mainly by the pattern of its plumage.

Lizard This breed and its close, and now extinct, relation, the London Fancy, are the only two breeds that have been cultivated for feather pattern. The London Fancy, which died out during the First World War, was clear-bodied with black wings and tail but was genetically a dark self. The Lizard also has black wings and tail, but apart from a crown of light feathers on its head called 'the cap', it is a dark bird, displaying rows of spangles on its back.

Clear Cap Silver Lizard cock

The early days of the canary fancy are not well documented, but it is certain that the Lizard has remained unchanged for at least 150 years and the factors that give rise to its unique characteristics – cap, spangle and black flight feathers – are not possessed by any other canary; it must not therefore be crossed with any other variety.

Lizards are colour-fed for exhibition and are generally regarded as one-year show birds, as their black flights are replaced by grizzled feathers in their second year.

Canary mules

This term refers to the offspring produced by cross breeding between a canary and a British finch. Not all finches are willing partners, but it has long been known that certain species, of which the goldfinch, linnet, bullfinch and greenfinch are most frequently used, when mated to a canary, produce hybrids that display characteristics of both parents. Such crosses are invariably sterile and the practice cannot lead to the creation of fertile hybrids and thereby new species.

The first aim of mule breeders is to obtain young hybrids, for success is not easily achieved. It is usual

Greenfinch mule

practice to pair a cock finch to a canary hen; the male greenfinch however is a somewhat unreliable hybridizer, while the cock bullfinch has never fertilized a canary's eggs; it is therefore sensible to employ the hens of these two finches as partners to a cock canary. Any type of canary can be used for mule breeding, but to obtain young of exhibition quality, a Norwich is the most suitable.

Learn from experience British finches tend to come into breeding condition later in spring than canaries, and they have their own preferences with regard to feeding that must be observed. The fancier needs to know each bird's requirements and though general management techniques during the breeding season are broadly similar to those employed for canaries, results can be unpredictable and pairs require much more individual attention. An understanding of the habits of finches and their nesting preferences is useful; their relationship with a domesticated canary, however, is something that can be learnt only through experience.

Mules on show A good mule will always attract attention on the show bench and the rewards for a successful exhibitor can be high. The judge will look for a large, shapely cock bird, possessing glowing colour and clearly demonstrating its parentage. Most mules have dark plumage, but very occasionally a clear, or a clear bird with even wing markings, is bred, and when such an exhibit has the requisite finch type, with a Norwich canary's size and colour, it is very highly prized indeed. An added bonus, though not to an exhibitor, is that cock linnet mules are often very sweet songsters and at one time were in great demand as pets.

Anyone who contemplates taking up this fascinating branch of the fancy should get in touch with a mule enthusiast and find out at first hand exactly what is involved. It is also important to understand the laws about keeping native birds captive in Britain. Nowadays only a strictly limited range of species may be bought and sold, and the birds must have been bred in captivity and close-rung (marked with a special type of ring that indicates their captive status).

Aviaries

If your intention is not to exhibit but simply to keep a number of canaries for their beauty and song, you can house them in an aviary.

Construction

As it is made mainly of wire netting or wire mesh, the cost of such a structure will be much less than that of a bird room, and if it is to be used during the summer months only, you need cover just a small part of the roof and sides to give protection from wind and rain.

If, however, the aviary is to be the birds' permanent home, you must add a weather- and frost-proof shelter, to which the inmates can retire during very bad weather. The choice of site is often limited, but if possible it should be an open sunny situation and not beneath overhanging tree branches.

To avoid being blown over in storms, the aviary should be securely attached to its base, and in this case an excellent base is concrete, or even paving stones set in a bed of sand.

Inmates

Providing the aviary is large enough, other species of comparable size and temperament may be included to form a mixed collection. Attempts to breed will inevitably take place in the spring and though there can be no control over matings, canaries will nest quite happily in such conditions. However, it is sensible to keep a ratio of one cock bird to three hens, to minimize squabbling and to provide ample cover for nesting sites, by means of bunches of twigs and heather.

Management

In a small aviary (one with a ground area of less than 7.5 sq m/80 sq ft) any attempt to grow plants will be foiled by the birds and a natural earth or grass floor will become fouled and sour. A solid or gravel floor covering which can be washed down or raked clean is therefore preferable.

An ideal aviary for a number of canaries is escape-proof, provides places to perch, natural if possible, and shelter

If small bushes or plants are to be introduced, they should be in tubs which can be taken out and changed at intervals. Creepers planted outside the aviary and then trained up the wire sides can usually be successfully grown and will give cover and attract insects on which the birds may feed.

Take great care to exclude vermin, and for an aviary with an earth floor the netting should be buried at least 22 cm (9 in) deep and turned outwards for a further 7.5 cm (3 in) beneath the soil. All seed hoppers must also be placed in positions that are inaccessible to mice and sheltered from the elements.

Index

Photographic acknowledgments
Dennis Avon 35, 36; C. B. Studios 41, 49 top and bottom, 56; Bruce Coleman – Hans Reinhard 12–13, 52–53; M. Scott 28, 43

Illustrations by Linden Artists Ltd (David Webb and Martin Camm)